Dedicated to

My Neela Bunny and Priya Bear. I love you so much.

This book was made possible by the generous support of Kickstarter contributors. Many thanks to everyone who contributed to and encouraged this project.

First Edition
Printed and bound in China.
ISBN 978-0-9978790-0-1

NeelaGoestoSF.com

Neela Goes to
SAN FRANCISCO

A COUNTING BOOK

Written and illustrated by **MEENAL PATEL**

|

MASI (MA-SEE)

Hindi and Gujarati word for aunt,
specifically, a sister of the child's mom.

Many Indian languages have a special
title for each relationship in one's life.

This is Neela. She loves her cuddly Bear-Bear and learning about new places. Neela, Mommy and Daddy are going on an adventure to visit Meenal Masi and Uncle Day-Day in San Francisco.

San Francisco is a foggy city by the Pacific Ocean with a big bridge that stretches across the Golden Gate. One, two, three, weeeeeee! The plane flies up, down and through the clouds.

HOW MANY PLANES DO YOU SEE?

1

They bring suitcases packed full of clothes, snacks, books . . . and Bear-Bear too!

HOW MANY SUITCASES DO YOU SEE?

Meenal Masi and Uncle Day-Day live in an apartment surrounded by pretty Victorian houses. The houses sit right next to each other and are painted in every color.

HOW MANY HOUSES DO YOU SEE?

From the apartment window, Neela and Bear-Bear can see a cable car rolling along and speedy cars zooming by. They are excited to explore the city.

HOW MANY CARS DO YOU SEE?

4

They go to Chinatown, where they wander through markets and see hundreds of colorful paper lanterns hanging across all the streets.

HOW MANY LANTERNS DO YOU SEE?

5

They have a lot of tea parties, including one at the Japanese Tea Garden where Bear-Bear eats so many tea cookies. Oh my!

HOW MANY COOKIES DO YOU SEE?

They go to Fisherman's Wharf and see the sea lions swimming and flip-flopping around Pier 39.

HOW MANY SEA LIONS DO YOU SEE?

They walk up and down and all around
San Francisco's steep and curvy hills.
As they walk, Neela finds a giant leaf
that is as big as her head!

HOW MANY LEAVES DO YOU SEE?

8

They walk around Golden Gate Park,
where they see tall redwood trees,
botanical gardens and windmills.

HOW MANY TREES DO YOU SEE?

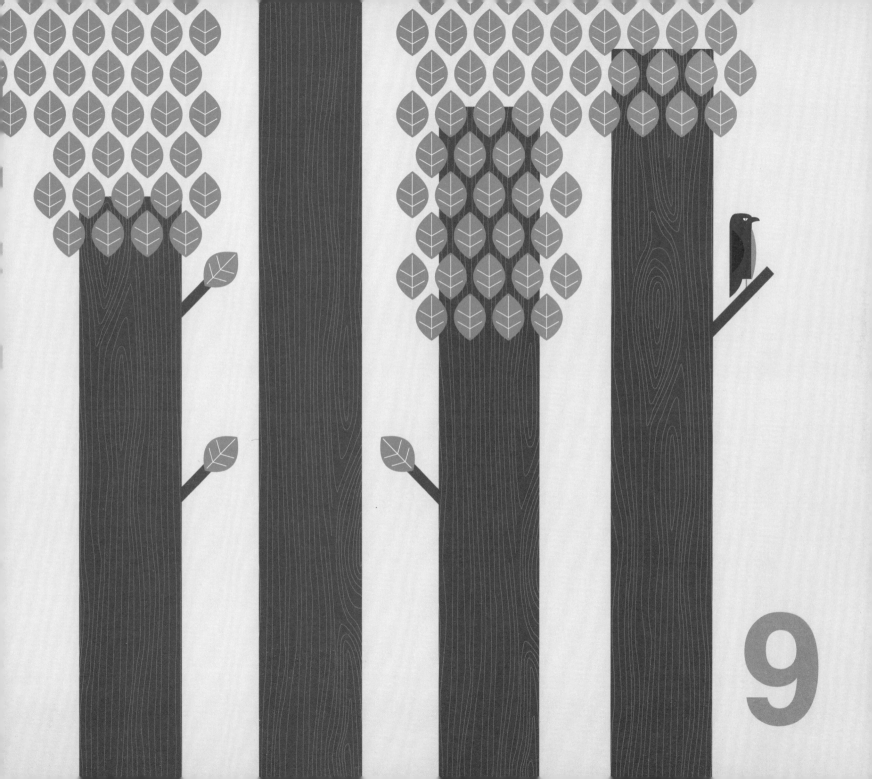

And they see puppies running, jumping and playing on the big hill at Alamo Square Park.

HOW MANY PUPPIES DO YOU SEE?

WOOF WOOF

GOLDEN
GATE
BRIDGE

San Francisco

CITY BY THE BAY

CALIFORNIA

Pacific Ocean

N

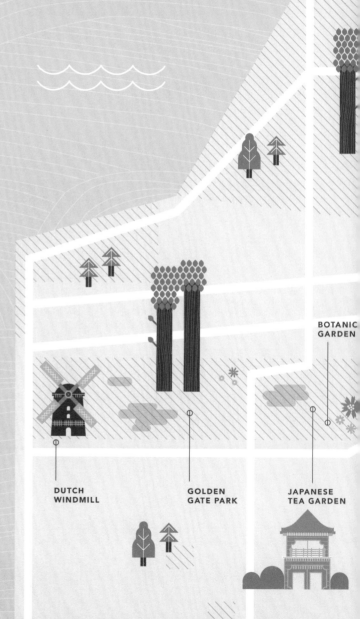

BOTANIC
GARDEN

DUTCH
WINDMILL

GOLDEN
GATE PARK

JAPANESE
TEA GARDEN

ALCATRAZ
ISLAND

TREASURE
ISLAND

FISHERMAN'S
WHARF

PALACE OF
FINE ARTS

LOMBARD
STREET

PIER 39

BAY BRIDGE

POWELL-HYDE
CABLE CAR

CHINATOWN

ALAMO
SQUARE

FERRY
BUILDING

UTRO
OWER

San Francisco Bay

Happy Adventuring!

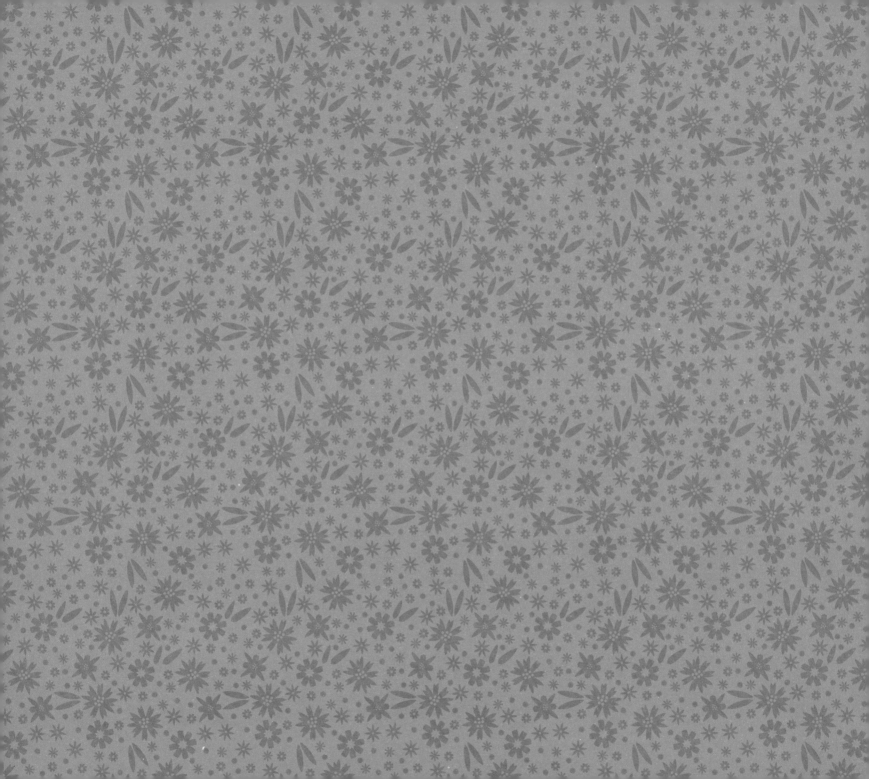